Christmas Memories

Our Family Christmas Journal

O Christmas! Merry Christmas!
Is it really come again?

Brownlow

Brownlow Publishing Company, Inc.

Christmas Bells

$\mathcal{I}$ heard the bells on Christmas Day
Their old, familiar carols play,
And wild and sweet the words repeat
Of peace on earth, good-will to men.

Henry Wadsworth Longfellow

Christmas Skating ISBN: 1-57051-073-3
Girls With Tree ISBN: 1-57051-025-3
Victorian Angel ISBN: 1-57051-024-5
Fireside Edition ISBN: 1-57051-167-5

Cover/Interior: Koechel Peterson & Associates

Printed in USA

A Treasure of
Special Christmas Memories
of the

_____

Family

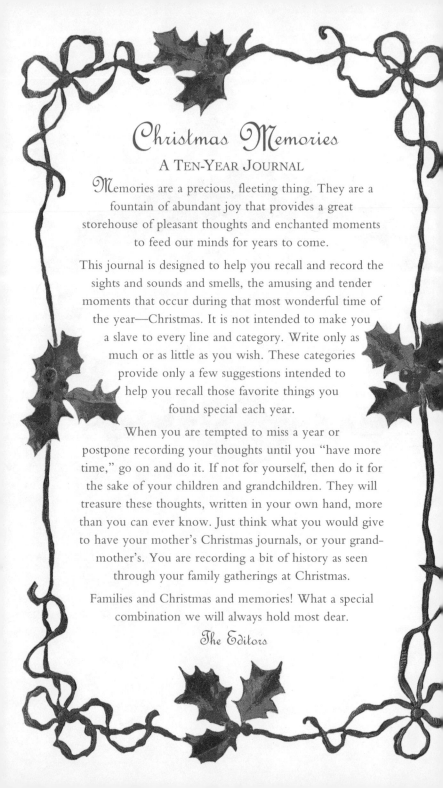

Christmas Memories

A Ten-Year Journal

Memories are a precious, fleeting thing. They are a fountain of abundant joy that provides a great storehouse of pleasant thoughts and enchanted moments to feed our minds for years to come.

This journal is designed to help you recall and record the sights and sounds and smells, the amusing and tender moments that occur during that most wonderful time of the year—Christmas. It is not intended to make you a slave to every line and category. Write only as much or as little as you wish. These categories provide only a few suggestions intended to help you recall those favorite things you found special each year.

When you are tempted to miss a year or postpone recording your thoughts until you "have more time," go on and do it. If not for yourself, then do it for the sake of your children and grandchildren. They will treasure these thoughts, written in your own hand, more than you can ever know. Just think what you would give to have your mother's Christmas journals, or your grand-mother's. You are recording a bit of history as seen through your family gatherings at Christmas.

Families and Christmas and memories! What a special combination we will always hold most dear.

The Editors

The Friendly Beasts

Jesus our Brother, kind and good,
Was humbly born in a stable rude,
And the friendly beasts around Him stood;
Jesus our Brother, kind and good.

"I," said the donkey, shaggy and brown,
"I carried His mother up hill and down;
I carried His mother to Bethlehem town.
I," said the donkey, shaggy and brown.

"I," said the cow, all white and red,
"I gave Him my manger for His bed;
I gave Him my hay to pillow His head.
I," said the cow, all white and red.

"I," said the sheep, with the curly horn,
"I gave Him wool for His blanket warm;
He wore my coat on Christmas morn.
I," said the sheep, with the curly horn.

"I," said the dove from the rafters high,
"Cooed Him to sleep that He should not cry;
We cooed Him to sleep, my mate and I.
I," said the dove from the rafters high.

Thus ev'ry beast by some good spell,
In the stable dark was glad to tell
Of the gift he gave Emmanuel,
The gift he gave Emmanuel.

Medieval French Christmas Carol

Christmas Memories
for the Year _____

Our Family Gathered at

_____
_____
_____
_____

Those Present Were

_____
_____
_____
_____

New Members of the Family
Since Last Christmas

_____
_____
_____
_____

Special Traditions We Enjoy Each Year

_____

_____

_____

_____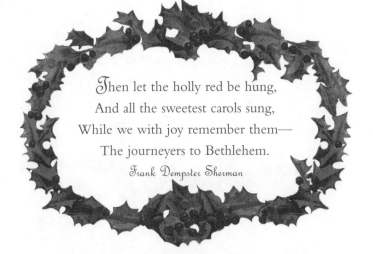

New Traditions We Started

_____

_____

_____

_____ ✠

Then let the holly red be hung,
And all the sweetest carols sung,
While we with joy remember them—
The journeyers to Bethlehem.

Frank Dempster Sherman

Special Activities of Christmas Eve

_____

_____

_____

_____

_____

_____

_____

_____

_____

Far, far away is Bethlehem,
and years are long and dim,
Since Mary held the Holy Child
and angels sang for Him.
But still to hearts where love and faith
make room for Christ in them,
He comes again, the Child from God,
to find His Bethlehem.

W. Russell Bowie

Special Activities of Christmas Day

_____
_____
_____
_____
_____
_____
_____

Our Christmas Day Menu

_____
_____
_____
_____
_____
_____
_____
_____

Special Gifts—
Both Given and Received

_____
_____
_____
_____
_____
_____
_____
_____
_____
_____
_____
_____
_____
_____
_____
_____
_____

New Ornaments and Decorations for the Tree and House

_____

_____

_____

Special Guests During the Holidays

_____

_____

_____

_____

Of course God might have chosen other methods.
He might have sent forth His Son trailing clouds
of glory from the opened heavens with a legion of angels
for His bodyguard. Or He might have revealed
His presence by one of those strange and startling theophanies
which are occasionally recorded in the Old Testament.
He might have heralded His coming with earthquake, tempest,
or the voice of thunder. But no! A baby is
born of a humble girl in the outhouse of a crowded inn;
and Love has set forth on His mighty mission.

Edward Gibbon

Favorite Plays, Movies, Concerts of the Season

_____
_____
_____
_____
_____
_____

Special Spiritual Emphasis This Christmas

_____
_____
_____
_____
_____
_____

Photo of Our Family This Year

Whatever else be lost among the years,
Let us keep Christmas still a shining thing:
Whatever doubts assail us, or what fears,
Let us hold close one day, remembering
Its poignant meaning for the hearts of men.
Let us get back our childlike faith again.

Grace Noll Crowell

"While Sheperds Watched Their Flocks by Night

Like small curled feathers, white and soft,
The little clouds went by,
Across the moon, and past the stars,
And down the western sky:
In upland pastures, where the grass
With frosted dew was white,
Like snowy clouds the young sheep lay,
That first, best Christmas night.

The shepherds slept; and, glimmering faint,
With twist of thin, blue smoke,
Only their fire's crackling flames
The tender silence broke—
Save when a young lamb raised his head,
Or, when the night wind blew,
A nesting bird would softly stir,
Where dusky olives grew—

With finger on her solemn lip,
Night hushed the shadowy earth,
And only stars and angels saw
The little Saviour's birth;

Then came such flash of silver light
Across the bending skies,
The wondering shepherds woke, and hid
Their frightened dazzled eyes!

And all their gentle sleepy flock
Looked up, then slept again,
Nor knew the light that dimmed the stars
Brought endless peace to men—
Nor even heard the gracious words
That down the ages ring—
"The Christ is born! the Lord has come,
Good-will on earth to bring!"

Then o'er the moonlit, misty fields,
Dumb with the world's great joy,
The shepherds sought the white-walled town,
Where lay the baby boy—
And oh, the gladness of the world,
The glory of the skies,
Because the longed-for Christ looked up
In Mary's happy eyes!

Margaret Deland

Christmas Memories
for the Year _____

Our Family Gathered at

_____
_____
_____
_____

Those Present Were

_____
_____
_____
_____

New Members of the Family
Since Last Christmas

_____
_____
_____
_____

Special Traditions We Enjoy Each Year

_____
_____
_____
_____

New Traditions We Started

_____
_____
_____
_____

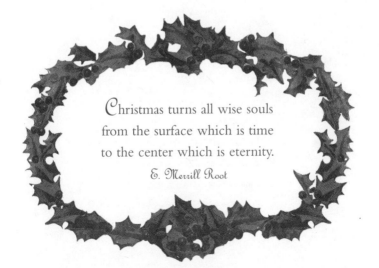

Christmas turns all wise souls
from the surface which is time
to the center which is eternity.

E. Merrill Root

Special Activities of Christmas Eve

_____

_____

_____

_____

_____

_____

_____

_____

_____

They were all looking for a king
To slay their foes and lift them high.
Thou cam'st, a little baby thing
That made a woman cry.
O Son of Man, to right my lot
Naught but Thy presence can avail;
Yet on the road Thy wheels are not
Nor on the sea Thy sail.
My how or when Thou wilt not heed,
But come down Thine own secret stair,
That Thou may'st answer all my need,
Yea, every bygone prayer.

George MacDonald

Special Activities of Christmas Day

_____
_____
_____
_____
_____
_____
_____
_____

Our Christmas Day Menu

_____
_____
_____
_____
_____
_____
_____
_____

Special Gifts—
Both Given and Received

_____
_____
_____
_____
_____
_____
_____
_____
_____
_____
_____
_____
_____
_____
_____
_____
_____

New Ornaments and Decorations for the Tree and House

_____

_____

_____

Special Guests During the Holidays

_____

_____

_____

Mother's gift to Father was yearly the same but always
received by him with surprise and gratitude. She made him
slippers of cross-stitched wool which, when completed,
she took to our good old cobbler who attached leather soles and
heels to the embroidered wool uppers. Mother had obtained the
design of crimson roses and green leaves on a black wool
background many years before from _Godey's Lady's Book_
and felt it could not be improved upon. Father often remarked
that they gave him perfect comfort and proved it by wearing
them in the evening and all relaxed hours.

Polly McKean Bell, Portland, Oregon, 1880s

Favorite Plays, Movies, Concerts of the Season

_____
_____
_____
_____
_____
_____
_____

Special Spiritual Emphasis This Christmas

_____
_____
_____
_____
_____
_____
_____

Photo of our Family This Year

Roses may come
and roses may go,
But Christmas brings
the mistletoe.

Christmas Memories
for the Year _____

Our Family Gathered at

_____
_____
_____
_____

Those Present Were

_____
_____
_____
_____

New Members of the Family
Since Last Christmas

_____
_____
_____
_____

Special Traditions We Enjoy Each Year

_____
_____
_____
_____

New Traditions We Started

_____
_____
_____
_____

Away in a manger, no crib for a bed,
The little Lord Jesus laid down His sweet head.
The stars in the sky looked down where He lay,
The little Lord Jesus, asleep on the hay.

Martin Luther

Special Activities of Christmas Eve

_____

_____

_____

_____

_____

_____

_____

_____

_____

A Christmas Carol

There's a song in the air!
There's a star in the sky!
There's a mother's deep prayer
And a baby's low cry!
And the star rains its fire while the Beautiful sing,
For the manger of Bethlehem cradles a king.

There's a tumult of joy
O'er the wonderful birth,
For the virgin's sweet boy
Is the Lord of the earth,
Ay! the star rains its fire and the Beautiful sing,
For the manger of Bethlehem cradles a king!

Josiah Gilbert Holland

Special Activities of Christmas Day

_____
_____
_____
_____
_____
_____
_____
_____

Our Christmas Day Menu

_____
_____
_____
_____
_____
_____
_____
_____

Special Gifts—
Both Given and Received

_____

_____

_____

_____

_____

_____

_____

_____

_____

_____

_____

_____

_____

_____

_____

_____

New Ornaments and Decorations for the Tree and House

_____

_____

_____

Special Guests During the Holidays

_____

_____

_____

_____

Behold a simple, tender Babe, in freezing winter night,
In homely manger trembling lies;
Alas! a piteous sight.

The inns are full; no man will yield this little Pilgrim bed;
But forced he is with silly beasts
In crib to shroud his head.

Despise him not for lying there; first what he is inquire:
An Orient pearl is often found
In depth of dirty mire.

Robert Southwell

Favorite Plays, Movies, Concerts
of the Season

_____
_____
_____
_____
_____
_____
_____

Special Spiritual Emphasis This
Christmas

_____
_____
_____
_____
_____
_____
_____

Photo of Our Family This Year

$\mathcal{I}$ will honor Christmas in my heart
and try to keep it all the year.

Charles Dickens

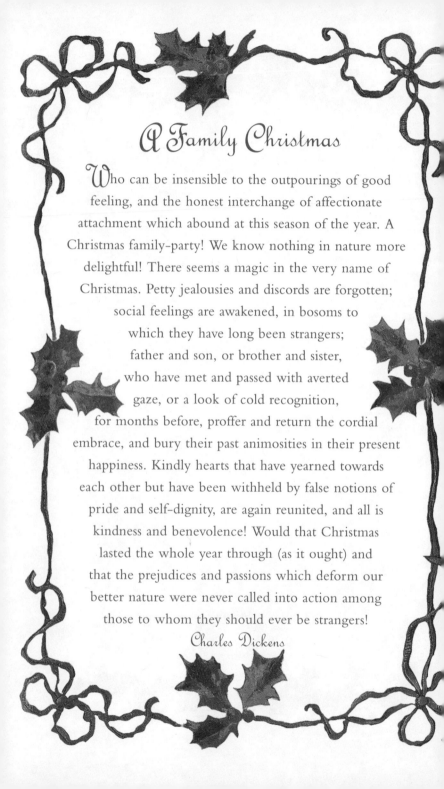

A Family Christmas

Who can be insensible to the outpourings of good
feeling, and the honest interchange of affectionate
attachment which abound at this season of the year. A
Christmas family-party! We know nothing in nature more
delightful! There seems a magic in the very name of
Christmas. Petty jealousies and discords are forgotten;
social feelings are awakened, in bosoms to
which they have long been strangers;
father and son, or brother and sister,
who have met and passed with averted
gaze, or a look of cold recognition,
for months before, proffer and return the cordial
embrace, and bury their past animosities in their present
happiness. Kindly hearts that have yearned towards
each other but have been withheld by false notions of
pride and self-dignity, are again reunited, and all is
kindness and benevolence! Would that Christmas
lasted the whole year through (as it ought) and
that the prejudices and passions which deform our
better nature were never called into action among
those to whom they should ever be strangers!

Charles Dickens

The Shepherds Had an Angel

The shepherds had an angel,
The wise men had a star,
But what have I, a little child,
To guide me home from far,
Where glad stars sing together,
And singing angels are?

Lord Jesus is my Guardian,
So I can nothing lack;
The lambs lie in His bosom
Along life's dangerous track:
The wilful lambs that go astray
He, bleeding, fetches back.

Lord, bring me nearer day by day,
Till I my voice unite,
And sing my 'Glory, glory,'
With angels clad in white,
All 'Glory, glory,' given to Thee,
Through all the heavenly height.

Christina Georgina Rossetti

Christmas Memories
for the Year _____

Our Family Gathered at

_____
_____
_____
_____

Those Present Were

_____
_____
_____
_____

New Members of the Family
Since Last Christmas

_____
_____
_____
_____

Special Traditions We Enjoy Each Year

_____

_____

_____

_____

New Traditions We Started

_____

_____

_____

_____

May joy come from heaven above
To all those who Christmas love.

19th-Century Christmas Card

Special Activities of Christmas Eve

_____

_____

_____

_____

_____

_____

_____

_____

_____

Let not our hearts be busy inns,
That have no room for Thee,
But cradles for the living Christ
And His nativity.

Still driven by a thousand cares
The pilgrims come and go;
The hurried caravans press on;
The inns are crowded so!

Oh, lest we starve, and lest we die,
In our stupidity,
Come, Holy Child, within and share
Our hospitality.

Ralph Cushman

Special Activities of Christmas Day

_____
_____
_____
_____
_____
_____
_____

Our Christmas Day Menu

_____
_____
_____
_____
_____
_____
_____
_____

Special Gifts—
  Both Given and Received

_____
_____
_____
_____
_____
_____
_____
_____
_____
_____
_____
_____
_____
_____
_____
_____

New Ornaments and Decorations for the Tree and House

_____

_____

_____

Special Guests During the Holidays

_____

_____

_____

_____

Angels, from the realms of glory,
Wing your flight o'er all the earth,
Ye who sang creation's story,
Now proclaim Messiah's birth;
Come and worship,
Worship Christ the new-born King.

Shepherds, in the field abiding,
Watching o'er your flocks by night,
God with man is now residing,
Yonder shines the infant-light;
Come and worship,
Worship Christ the new-born King.

James Montgomery

Favorite Plays, Movies, Concerts of the Season

_____
_____
_____
_____
_____
_____
_____

Special Spiritual Emphasis This Christmas

_____
_____
_____
_____
_____
_____
_____

Photo of Our Family This Year

Heap on more wood!—the wind is chill;
But let it whistle as it will,
We'll keep our Christmas merry still.

Sir Walter Scott

Christmas Memories
for the Year _____

Our Family Gathered at

_____
_____
_____
_____

Those Present Were

_____
_____
_____
_____

New Members of the Family
Since Last Christmas

_____
_____
_____
_____

Special Traditions We Enjoy Each Year

_____

_____

_____

_____

New Traditions We Started

_____

_____

_____

_____

The world is waiting in the snow
As white as white can be,
Is waiting for the coming
Of Christ's nativity.

19th-Century Christmas Card

Special Activities of Christmas Eve

_____

_____

_____

_____

_____

_____

_____

_____

_____

It is the calm and solemn night!
A thousand bells ring out, and throw
Their joyous peals abroad, and smite
The darkness—charmed and holy now!
The night that erst no name had worn,
To it a happy name is given;
For in that stable lay, new-born,
The peaceful prince of earth and heaven,
In the solemn midnight,
Centuries ago!

Alfred Dommett

Special Activities of Christmas Day

_____

_____

_____

_____

_____

_____

_____

Our Christmas Day Menu

_____

_____

_____

_____

_____

_____

_____

_____

Special Gifts—
Both Given and Received

_____

_____

_____

_____

_____

_____

_____

_____

_____

_____

_____

_____

_____

_____

_____

_____

_____

New Ornaments and Decorations for the Tree and House

_____

_____

_____

Special Guests During the Holidays

_____

_____

_____

_____

A Merrie Christmas

"A merrie Christmas" to you!
For we serve the Lord with mirth,
And we carol forth glad tidings
Of our holy Saviour's birth.
So we keep the olden greeting
With its meaning deep and true,
And with "a merrie Christmas"
And a happy New Year to you!

Frances Ridley Havergal

Favorite Plays, Movies, Concerts of the Season

_____

_____

_____

_____

_____

_____

_____

Special Spiritual Emphasis This Christmas

_____

_____

_____

_____

_____

_____

_____

Photo of Our Family This Year

He who has not Christmas in his
heart will never find it under a tree.

Roy L. Smith

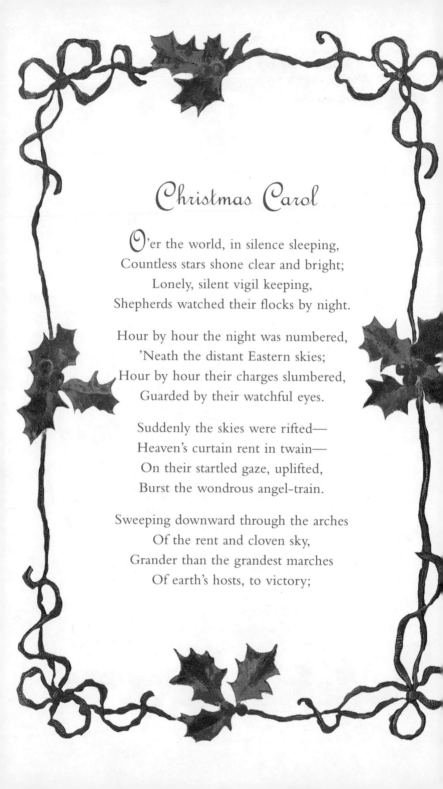

Christmas Carol

O'er the world, in silence sleeping,
Countless stars shone clear and bright;
Lonely, silent vigil keeping,
Shepherds watched their flocks by night.

Hour by hour the night was numbered,
'Neath the distant Eastern skies;
Hour by hour their charges slumbered,
Guarded by their watchful eyes.

Suddenly the skies were rifted—
Heaven's curtain rent in twain—
On their startled gaze, uplifted,
Burst the wondrous angel-train.

Sweeping downward through the arches
Of the rent and cloven sky,
Grander than the grandest marches
Of earth's hosts, to victory;

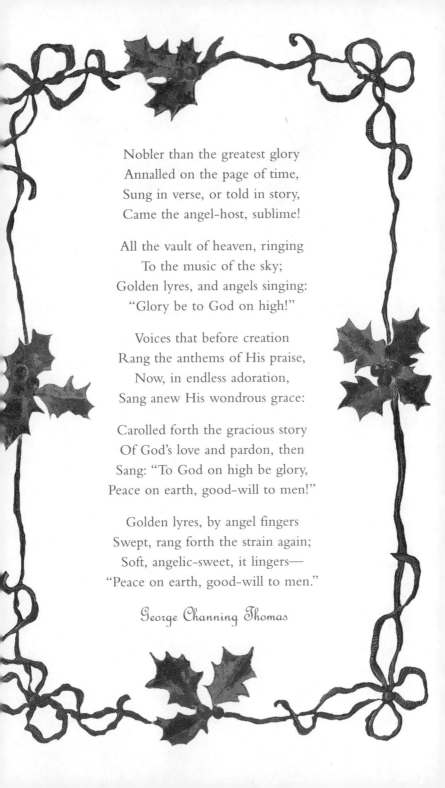

Nobler than the greatest glory
Annalled on the page of time,
Sung in verse, or told in story,
Came the angel-host, sublime!

All the vault of heaven, ringing
To the music of the sky;
Golden lyres, and angels singing:
"Glory be to God on high!"

Voices that before creation
Rang the anthems of His praise,
Now, in endless adoration,
Sang anew His wondrous grace:

Carolled forth the gracious story
Of God's love and pardon, then
Sang: "To God on high be glory,
Peace on earth, good-will to men!"

Golden lyres, by angel fingers
Swept, rang forth the strain again;
Soft, angelic-sweet, it lingers—
"Peace on earth, good-will to men."

George Channing Thomas

Christmas Memories
for the Year _____

Our Family Gathered at

_____
_____
_____
_____

Those Present Were

_____
_____
_____
_____

New Members of the Family
Since Last Christmas

_____
_____
_____
_____

Special Traditions We Enjoy Each Year

_____

_____

_____

_____

New Traditions We Started

_____

_____

_____

_____

A Christmas candle is a lovely thing;
It makes no noise at all,
But softly gives itself away;
While quite unselfish, it grows small.

Eva K. Logue.

Special Activities of Christmas Eve

_____

_____

_____

_____

_____

_____

_____

_____

_____

Not to those in soft apparel,
Was the Savior first made known;
Not to noble or to high-born,
Or to courtiers round a throne;
Not to kings or mighty monarchs,
Was the King of Kings revealed,
But to poor and lonely shepherds
In the lonely pasture field.

Special Activities of Christmas Day

_____

_____

_____

_____

_____

_____

_____

Our Christmas Day Menu

_____

_____

_____

_____

_____

_____

_____

_____

Special Gifts—
  Both Given and Received

_____
_____
_____
_____
_____
_____
_____
_____
_____
_____
_____
_____
_____
_____
_____
_____

New Ornaments and Decorations for the Tree and House

_____

_____

_____

Special Guests During the Holidays

_____

_____

_____

_____

A merry Christmas morning
To each and every one!
The rose has kissed the dawning
And the gold is in the sun.
And may the Christmas splendor
A joyous greeting bear,
Of love that's true and tender
And faith that's sweet and fair!

Favorite Plays, Movies, Concerts of the Season

_____
_____
_____
_____
_____
_____
_____

Special Spiritual Emphasis This Christmas

_____
_____
_____
_____
_____
_____
_____

Photo of Our Family This Year

O Father, may that Holy star
Grow every year more bright,
And send its glorious beams afar
To fill the world with light.

William Cullen Bryant

Christmas Memories
for the Year _____

Our Family Gathered at

_____

_____

_____

_____

Those Present Were

_____

_____

_____

_____

New Members of the Family
Since Last Christmas

_____

_____

_____

_____

Special Traditions We Enjoy Each Year

_____
_____
_____
_____

New Traditions We Started

_____
_____
_____
_____

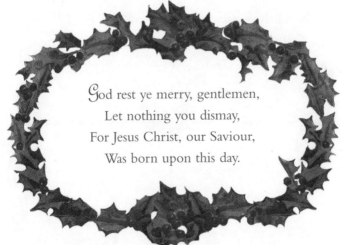

God rest ye merry, gentlemen,
Let nothing you dismay,
For Jesus Christ, our Saviour,
Was born upon this day.

Special Activities of Christmas Eve

_____

_____

_____

_____

_____

_____

_____

_____

_____

Everywhere—everywhere, Christmas tonight!
Christmas in lands of the fir tree and pine,
Christmas in lands of the palm tree and vine,
Christmas where snow peaks stand solemn and white,
Christmas where corn fields lie sunny and bright,
Everywhere, everywhere, Christmas tonight.

Phillips Brooks

Special Activities of Christmas Day

_____
_____
_____
_____
_____
_____
_____
_____

Our Christmas Day Menu

_____
_____
_____
_____
_____
_____
_____
_____

Special Gifts—
Both Given and Received

_____
_____
_____
_____
_____
_____
_____
_____
_____
_____
_____
_____
_____
_____
_____
_____
_____

New Ornaments and Decorations for the Tree and House

_____

_____

_____

Special Guests During the Holidays

_____

_____

_____

_____

A Christmas Prayer

O God, our loving Father,
help us rightly to remember the birth of Jesus,
that we may share in the song of the angels,
the gladness of the shepherds,
and the worship of the Wise Men.
May the Christmas morning make us
happy to be your children
and the Christmas evening bring us
to our bed with grateful thoughts,
forgiving and forgiven,
for Jesus' sake. Amen.

Robert Louis Stevenson

Favorite Plays, Movies, Concerts of the Season

_____
_____
_____
_____
_____
_____
_____

Special Spiritual Emphasis This Christmas

_____
_____
_____
_____
_____
_____
_____

Photo of Our Family This Year

Song of Bethlehem

O sing a song of Bethlehem,
Of shepherds watching there,
And of the news that came to them
From angels in the air:
The light that shone on Bethlehem
Fills all the world today;
Of Jesus' birth and peace on earth
The angels sing alway.

Louis F. Benson

Cradle Hymn

Hush, my dear, lie still and slumber;
Holy angels guard thy bed;
Heavenly blessings without number
Gently falling on thy head.

Sleep, my babe, thy food and raiment,
House and home, thy friends provide;
All without thy care, or payment,
All thy wants are well supplied.

How much better thou'rt attended
Than the Son of God could be,
When from heaven He descended,
And became a child like thee!

Soft and easy is thy cradle;
Coarse and hard thy Saviour lay,
When His birthplace was a stable,
And His softest bed was hay.

See the kindly shepherds round Him,
Telling wonders from the sky!
When they sought Him, there they found Him,
With His Virgin-Mother by.

See the lovely babe a-dressing;
Lovely infant, how He smiled!
When He wept, the mother's blessing
Soothed and hushed the holy child.

Lo, He slumbers in His manger,
Where the honest oxen fed;
—Peace, my darling! here's no danger!
Here's no ox a-near thy bed!

Mayst thou live to know and fear Him,
Trust and love Him all thy days;
Then go dwell forever near Him,
See His face, and sing His praise!

I could give thee thousand kisses,
Hoping what I most desire;
Not a mother's fondest wishes
Can to greater joys aspire.

Isaac Watts

Christmas Memories
for the Year _____

Our Family Gathered at

_____
_____
_____
_____

Those Present Were

_____
_____
_____
_____

New Members of the Family
 Since Last Christmas

_____
_____
_____
_____

Special Traditions We Enjoy Each Year

_____
_____
_____
_____

New Traditions We Started

_____
_____
_____
_____

With ivy and laurel,
And bright holly berry,
Be Christmas to you
Both happy and merry.

Special Activities of Christmas Eve

_____

_____

_____

_____

_____

_____

_____

_____

_____

_____

To be Himself a star most bright,

To bring the wise men to His sight,

To be Himself a voice most sweet,

To call the shepherds to His feet,

To be a child—it was His will,

That folk like us might find Him still.

John Erskine

Special Activities of Christmas Day

_____

_____

_____

_____

_____

_____

_____

Our Christmas Day Menu

_____

_____

_____

_____

_____

_____

_____

Special Gifts—
Both Given and Received

_____
_____
_____
_____
_____
_____
_____
_____
_____
_____
_____
_____
_____
_____
_____
_____

New Ornaments and Decorations for the Tree and House

_____

_____

_____

Special Guests During the Holidays

_____

_____

_____

Oh, let thy heart make melody,
And thankful songs uplift,
For Christ Himself is come to be
Thy glorious Christmas gift.

Frances Ridley Havergal

Favorite Plays, Movies, Concerts of the Season

_____
_____
_____
_____
_____
_____
_____

Special Spiritual Emphasis This Christmas

_____
_____
_____
_____
_____
_____
_____

Photo of Our Family This Year

The only real blind person at
Christmastime is he who has
not Christmas in his heart.

Helen Keller

Christmas Memories for the Year _____

Our Family Gathered at

_____
_____
_____
_____

Those Present Were

_____
_____
_____
_____

New Members of the Family Since Last Christmas

_____
_____
_____
_____

Special Traditions We Enjoy Each Year

_____

_____

_____

_____

New Traditions We Started

_____

_____

_____

_____

Angels and shepherds, birds of the sky,
Come where the Son of God doth lie;
Christ on the earth with man doth dwell,
Join in the shout, Noel, Noel.

Special Activities of Christmas Eve

Oh, Christmas is a jolly time
When forests hang with snow,
And other forests bend with toys,
And lordly Yule logs glow.

And Christmas is a solemn time
Because, beneath the star,
The first great Christmas Gift was given
To all men, near and far.

But not alone at Christmastime
Comes holiday and cheer,
For one who loves a little child
Hath Christmas all the year.

Florence Evelyn Pratt

Special Activities of Christmas Day

_____

_____

_____

_____

_____

_____

_____

Our Christmas Day Menu

_____

_____

_____

_____

_____

_____

_____

_____

Special Gifts—
Both Given and Received

_____
_____
_____
_____
_____
_____
_____
_____
_____
_____
_____
_____
_____
_____
_____
_____

New Ornaments and Decorations for the Tree and House

_____

_____

_____

Special Guests During the Holidays

_____

_____

_____

_____

Comes the Christ Child gentle
In December drear,
With deeds of loving-kindness
All the world to cheer.
May it be our endeavor—
Be we great or small—
To be like this dear Christ Child,
Kind to one and all.

Favorite Plays, Movies, Concerts of the Season

_____

_____

_____

_____

_____

_____

_____

Special Spiritual Emphasis This Christmas

_____

_____

_____

_____

_____

_____

_____

Photo of Our Family This Year

It is Christmas in the mansion,
Yule-log fires and silken frocks;
It is Christmas in the cottage,
Mother's filling little socks.

It is Christmas on the highway,
In the thronging, busy mart;
But the dearest, truest Christmas
Is the Christmas in the heart.

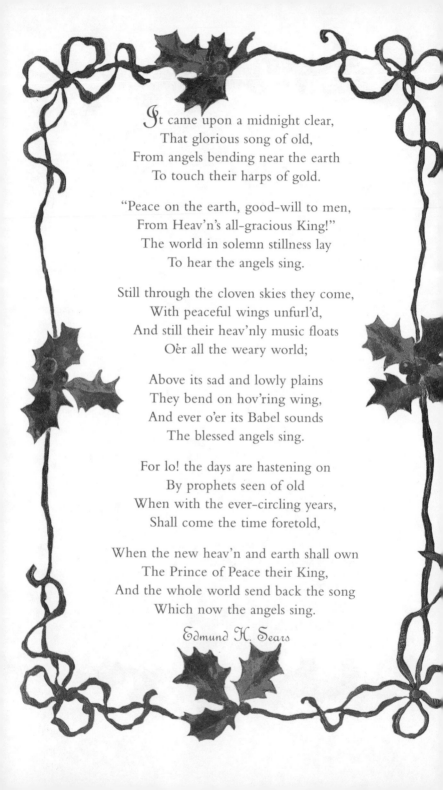

It came upon a midnight clear,
That glorious song of old,
From angels bending near the earth
To touch their harps of gold.

"Peace on the earth, good-will to men,
From Heav'n's all-gracious King!"
The world in solemn stillness lay
To hear the angels sing.

Still through the cloven skies they come,
With peaceful wings unfurl'd,
And still their heav'nly music floats
O'er all the weary world;

Above its sad and lowly plains
They bend on hov'ring wing,
And ever o'er its Babel sounds
The blessed angels sing.

For lo! the days are hastening on
By prophets seen of old
When with the ever-circling years,
Shall come the time foretold,

When the new heav'n and earth shall own
The Prince of Peace their King,
And the whole world send back the song
Which now the angels sing.

Edmund H. Sears

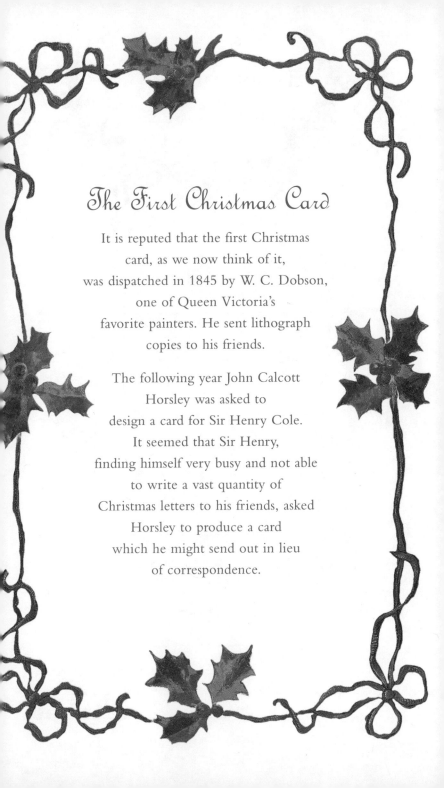

The First Christmas Card

It is reputed that the first Christmas
card, as we now think of it,
was dispatched in 1845 by W. C. Dobson,
one of Queen Victoria's
favorite painters. He sent lithograph
copies to his friends.

The following year John Calcott
Horsley was asked to
design a card for Sir Henry Cole.
It seemed that Sir Henry,
finding himself very busy and not able
to write a vast quantity of
Christmas letters to his friends, asked
Horsley to produce a card
which he might send out in lieu
of correspondence.

Christmas Memories
for the Year _____

Our Family Gathered at

_____
_____
_____
_____

Those Present Were

_____
_____
_____
_____

New Members of the Family
  Since Last Christmas

_____
_____
_____
_____

Special Traditions We Enjoy Each Year

_____

_____

_____

_____

New Traditions We Started

_____

_____

_____

_____

Come, Heavenly Child, and on this place
Shed the sweet halo of Thy grace.
O burning Love, O Heavenly Fire
Consume me with Thy deep desire.

Anna Hempstead Branch

Special Activities of Christmas Eve

There's more, much more, to Christmas
Than candlelight and cheer;
It's the spirit of sweet friendship,
That brightens all the year;
It's thoughtfulness and kindness,
It's hope reborn again,
For peace, for understanding
And for goodwill to men!

Special Activities of Christmas Day

_____
_____
_____
_____
_____
_____
_____
_____

Our Christmas Day Menu

_____
_____
_____
_____
_____
_____
_____
_____

Special Gifts—
Both Given and Received

_____
_____
_____
_____
_____
_____
_____
_____
_____
_____
_____
_____
_____
_____
_____
_____
_____

New Ornaments and Decorations for the Tree and House

_____

_____

_____

Special Guests During the Holidays

_____

_____

_____

_____

Come to the Manger

Come to the manger, come to the stall.

Come to the manger, come one and all.

Come to the manger by early morn.

Come to the manger; Jesus is born.

Favorite Plays, Movies, Concerts of the Season

_____

_____

_____

_____

_____

_____

_____

Special Spiritual Emphasis This Christmas

_____

_____

_____

_____

_____

_____

_____

Photo of Our Family This Year

Somehow not only for Christmas
but all the long year through,
The joy that you give others
is the joy that comes back to you.

John Greenleaf Whittier

Ye Ballad of Christmas

Sing a song of Christmas!
Pockets full of gold;
Plums and cakes for Polly's stocking,
More than it can hold.
Pudding in the great pot,
Turkey on the spit,
Merry faces round the fire,—
Smiling quite a bit!

Sing a song of Christmas!
Carols in the street,
People going home with bundles
Everywhere we meet.
Holly, fir, and spruce boughs
Green upon the wall,
Spotless snow upon the road,—
More about to fall.

Unknown

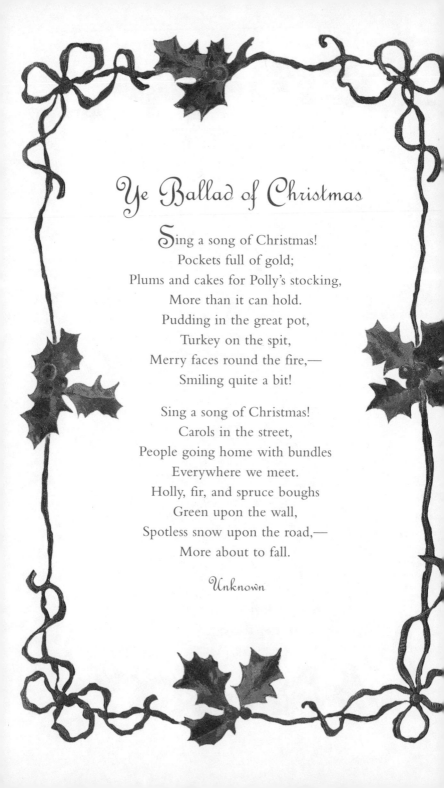